THE PETER RABBIT™ STENCIL BOOK

Devised by Jennie Walters

From the authorized and original tales™
BY **BEATRIX POTTER**

FREDERICK WARNE

Published by the Penguin Group
27 Wrights Lane, London W8 5TZ
Penguin Books USA Inc., 375 Hudson Street, New York, NY 10014, USA
Penguin Books Australia Ltd, Ringwood, Victoria, Australia
Penguin Books Canada Ltd, 10 Alcorn Avenue, Toronto, Ontario, Canada M4V 3B2
Penguin Books (NZ) Ltd, 182-190 Wairau Road, Auckland 10, New Zealand

Penguin Books Ltd, Registered Offices: Harmondsworth, Middlesex, England

First published 1993
1 3 5 7 9 10 8 6 4 2

Text copyright © Jennie Walters 1993
Illustrations by Colin Twinn and Piers Sandford
Copyright © Frederick Warne & Co., 1993

The Tale of Mrs. Tittlemouse copyright © Frederick Warne & Co., 1910, 1987

Other illustrations by Beatrix Potter copyright © Frederick Warne & Co., 1902, 1903,
1904, 1905, 1906, 1907, 1909, 1913, 1987

The Beatrix Potter character names and illustrations are trademarks of Frederick Warne

ISBN 0 7232 4046 9

Printed and bound in Hong Kong by Imago Publishing Limited.

THE TALE OF MRS. TITTLEMOUSE

Once upon a time there was a wood-mouse, and her name was Mrs. Tittlemouse.

She lived in a bank under a hedge.

Such a funny house! There were yards and yards of sandy passages, leading to storerooms and nut-cellars and seed-cellars, all amongst the roots of the hedge.

There was a kitchen, a parlour, a pantry, and a larder.

Also, there was Mrs. Tittlemouse's bedroom, where she slept in a little box bed!

Mrs. Tittlemouse was a most terribly tidy particular little mouse, always sweeping and dusting the soft sandy floors.

Sometimes a beetle lost its way in the passages.

"Shuh! shuh! little dirty feet!" said Mrs. Tittlemouse, clattering her dust-pan.

And one day a little old woman ran up and down in a red spotty cloak.

"Your house is on fire, Mother Ladybird! Fly away home to your children!"

Another day, a big fat spider came in to shelter from the rain.

"Beg pardon, is this not Miss Muffet's?"

"Go away, you bold bad spider! Leaving ends of cobweb all over my nice clean house!"

She bundled the spider out at a window.

He let himself down the hedge with a long thin bit of string.

Mrs. Tittlemouse went on her way to a distant storeroom, to fetch cherry-stones and thistle-down seed for dinner.

All along the passage she sniffed, and looked at the floor.

"I smell a smell of honey; is it the cowslips outside, in the hedge? I am sure I can see the marks of little dirty feet."

Suddenly round a corner, she met Babbitty Bumble - "Zizz, Bizz, Bizzz!" said the bumble bee.

Mrs. Tittlemouse looked at her severely. She wished that she had a broom.

"Good-day, Babbitty Bumble; I should be glad to buy some beeswax. But what are you doing down here? Why do you always come in at a window, and say Zizz, Bizz, Bizzz?" Mrs. Tittlemouse began to get cross.

"Zizz, Wizz, Wizzz!" replied Babbitty Bumble in a peevish squeak. She sidled down a passage, and disappeared into a storeroom which had been used for acorns.

Mrs. Tittlemouse had eaten the acorns before Christmas; the storeroom ought to have been empty.

But it was full of untidy dry moss.

Mrs. Tittlemouse began to pull out the moss. Three or four other bees put their

heads out, and buzzed fiercely.

"I am not in the habit of letting lodgings; this is an intrusion!" said Mrs. Tittlemouse. "I will have them turned out - " "Buzz! Buzz! Buzzz!" - "I wonder who would help me?" "Bizz, Wizz, Wizzz!"

- "I will not have Mr. Jackson; he never wipes his feet."

Mrs. Tittlemouse decided to leave the bees till after dinner.

When she got back to the parlour, she heard some one coughing in a fat voice; and there sat Mr. Jackson himself!

He was sitting all over a small rocking-chair, twiddling his thumbs and smiling, with his feet on the fender.

He lived in a drain below the hedge, in a very dirty wet ditch.

"How do you do, Mr. Jackson? Deary me, you have got very wet!"

"Thank you, thank you, thank you, Mrs. Tittlemouse! I'll sit awhile and dry myself," said Mr. Jackson.

He sat and smiled, and the water dripped off his coat tails. Mrs. Tittlemouse went round with a mop.

He sat such a while that he had to be asked if he would take some dinner?

First she offered him cherry-stones. "Thank you, thank you, Mrs. Tittlemouse! No teeth, no teeth, no teeth!" said Mr. Jackson.

He opened his mouth most unnecessarily wide; he certainly had not a tooth in his head.

Then she offered him thistle-down seed - "Tiddly, widdly, widdly! Pouff, pouff, puff!" said Mr. Jackson. He blew the thistle-down all over the room.

"Thank you, thank you, thank you, Mrs. Tittlemouse! Now what I really - *really* should like - would be a little dish of honey!"

"I am afraid I have not got any, Mr. Jackson," said Mrs. Tittlemouse.

"Tiddly, widdly, widdly, Mrs. Tittlemouse!" said the smiling Mr. Jackson, "I can *smell* it; that is why I came to call."

Mr. Jackson rose ponderously from the table, and began to look into the cupboards.

Mrs. Tittlemouse followed him with a dish-cloth, to wipe his large wet footmarks off the parlour floor.

When he had convinced himself that there was no honey in the cupboards, he began to walk down the passage.

"Indeed, indeed, you will stick fast, Mr. Jackson!"

"Tiddly, widdly, widdly, Mrs. Tittlemouse!"

First he squeezed into the pantry.

"Tiddly, widdly, widdly? no honey? no honey, Mrs. Tittlemouse?"

There were three creepy-crawly people hiding in the plate-rack. Two of them got away; but the littlest one he caught.

Then he squeezed into the larder. Miss Butterfly was tasting the sugar; but she flew away out of the window.

"Tiddly, widdly, widdly, Mrs. Tittlemouse; you seem to have plenty of visitors!"

"And without any invitation!" said Mrs. Thomasina Tittlemouse.

They went along the sandy passage - "Tiddly widdly -" "Buzz! Wizz! Wizz!"

He met Babbitty round a corner, and snapped her up, and put her down again.

"I do not like bumble bees. They are all over bristles," said Mr. Jackson, wiping his mouth with his coat-sleeve.

"Get out, you nasty old toad!" shrieked Babbity Bumble.

"I shall go distracted!" scolded Mrs. Tittlemouse.

She shut herself up in the nut-cellar while Mr. Jackson pulled out the bees-nest. He seemed to have no objection to stings.

When Mrs. Tittlemouse ventured to come out - everybody had gone away.

But the untidiness was something dreadful - "Never did I see such a mess - smears of honey; and moss, and thistle-down - and marks of big and little dirty feet - all over my nice clean house!"

She gathered up the moss and the remains of the beeswax.

Then she went out and fetched some twigs, to partly close up the front door.

"I will make it too small for Mr. Jackson!"

She fetched soft soap, and a flannel, and a new scrubbing brush from the storeroom. But she was too tired to do any more. First she fell asleep in her chair, and then she went to bed.

"Will it every be tidy again?" said poor Mrs. Tittlemouse.

Next morning she got up very early and began a spring cleaning which lasted a fortnight.

She swept, and scrubbed, and dusted; and she rubbed up the furniture with beeswax and polished her little tin spoons.

When it was all beautifully neat and clean, she gave a party to five other little mice, without Mr. Jackson.

He smelt the party and came up the bank, but he could not squeeze in at the door.

So they handed him out acorn-cupfuls of honey-dew through the window, and he was not at all offended.

He sat outside in the sun, and said - "Tiddly, widdly, widdly! Your very good health, Mrs. Tittlemouse!"

THE END

GINGER AND PICKLES CROSSWORD

See if you can fill in this crossword using the pictures
to help you solve some of the clues.

Down

1. Sally Henny Penny put her sale poster up against the _____ *(4)*
2. Mrs. Tiggy-winkle bought a bar of _____ to do her washing *(4)*
3. Ginger and Pickles had to eat their own goods when they were _____ *(5)*
4. Somewhere to keep your money when you go shopping (5)
5. Ginger is a yellow _____-cat *(3)*
6. Samuel Whiskers looks like a large mouse; he is a _____ *(3)*
7. Pickles tried to get a dog licence from the Post _____ *(6)*
8. When a piece of cheese is divided exactly in two, it is cut in _____ *(4)*
9. Mr. John Dormouse, the other shopkeeper, stayed in _____ when his customers came to complain *(3)*
10. The mice came to Mr. John Dormouse to buy _____ , which they lit when it was dark *(7)*
11. Ginger owns the village shop with his friend _____ (7)

Across

1. When Pickles is happy, he will _____ his tail *(3)*

2. Ginger and Pickles sell _____ , which makes things sweet *(5)*

3. Ginger and Pickles send out a _____ to their customers who have not paid *(3)*

4. *across and 12. across,* Samuel Whiskers stood _____ a box, to reach the _____ *(2, 7)*

5. Pickles wears an _____ to protect his clothes *(5)*

6. A sticky sweet which you chew *(6)*

7. Small furry cheese customers *(4)*

8. Sally Henny Penny is what kind of bird? *(3)*

9. When Pickles saw the policeman, he began to _____ at him *(4)*

10. A shopkeeper must _____ up the bill *(3)*

11. Sally Henny Penny insists on being paid in _____ *(3)*

12. *See 4. across*

Peter Rabbit Stencils

This book has six pages of stencils which you can use to make some lovely pictures of Peter Rabbit and his friends. We've already met Mrs. Tittlemouse; here are a few words about the other animals in case you haven't met them before.

PETER RABBIT AND BENJAMIN BUNNY

Peter Rabbit and Benjamin Bunny are cousins who get up to all sorts of mischief. One day Peter squeezed under the gate into Mr. McGregor's garden to eat the tasty vegetables there, but was discovered

and lost his jacket and shoes. Benjamin helped Peter to get back his clothes and they took home onions for Peter's mother in a red spotted handkerchief.

TOM KITTEN

Tom Kitten and his sisters, Mittens and Moppet, were washed, brushed and dressed in their best clothes by their mother, Tabitha Twitchit, who was expecting friends for tea. Once out in the garden, though, they didn't stay clean and tidy for long. Their smart clothes came off one by one, to be picked up by the Puddle-duck family and lost for ever in the pond.

MR. JEREMY FISHER

Mr. Jeremy Fisher, a frog who lives in a damp little house among the buttercups at the edge of a pond, was fishing for minnows one day on a lily-leaf boat when a huge trout seized him in its mouth! Luckily the trout didn't like the taste of his mackintosh and spat him out again.

MRS. TIGGY-WINKLE

When Lucie lost three handkerchiefs and a pinafore, she climbed up the hill to look for them and met Mrs. Tiggy-winkle, who washes and irons all the animals' clothes.

SQUIRREL NUTKIN

Squirrel Nutkin is another mischievous little creature. He prefers dancing and making up riddles to gathering nuts for the winter on Owl Island with the other squirrels. But when he jumped on the head of Old Brown, the owl, he really did go too far!

HUNCA MUNCA

Hunca Munca and her husband, Tom Thumb, are also known as the Two Bad Mice. They broke into the dolls' house, smashed the dolls' food and stole some of their furniture.

GINGER AND PICKLES' SHOP

Ginger, a yellow tomcat, and Pickles, a terrier, kept all kinds of things in their village shop, from handkerchiefs to sugar - there was something to please everybody - but nobody paid them on time!

PIGLING BLAND AND ALEXANDER

Eight little pigs make a very large family, so Aunt Pettitoes had to send Pigling Bland and Alexander to market, though neither of them managed to find their way there. Alexander was taken by a policeman after losing his special travelling papers, and Pigling met a lovely black pig, Pig-wig, who escaped with him 'over the hills and far away'.

JEMIMA PUDDLE-DUCK

Jemima nearly came to a dreadful end when she left the farm in her finest bonnet and shawl to look for a place to lay her eggs. The elegant gentleman with sandy whiskers whom she met seemed so helpful; surely he couldn't be a fox who wanted to make her the main course for dinner?

USING THE STENCILS

Carefully tear out the stencil pages from the centre of this book. Cut out each stencil, leaving as much solid card around it as possible.

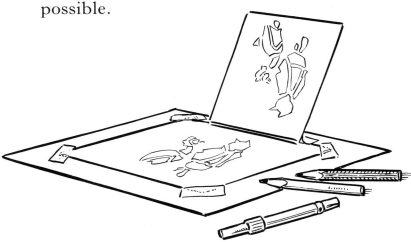

It's a good idea to stick the stencil to your paper with some masking tape (which you can take off again without tearing the paper) or a blob of display adhesive (Blu-tack) to each corner to stop the stencil slipping.

NB: When making any of the ideas in this book, it's useful to refer back to this section to help you.

STENCILLING METHODS

Painting and Colouring
Fix down your stencil (as suggested above) and draw around the inside of the stencil with pencil to create an outline. Then fill in the shapes with paints, coloured pens, or crayons once you've removed the stencil.

Alternatively you can colour directly through the stencil. Fix it down and colour through with chunky pens, wax crayons, or coloured pencils.

Stained Glass Pictures
Scribble over a piece of greaseproof or tracing paper with some wax crayons until you have an area as big as your stencil picture. Narrow stripes of bright colours will look good - try not to leave any spaces. Then paint over the wax crayon with a thin layer of black paint or ink.

When the paint is dry, lay over your stencil, fix it down and carefully scrape away the black paint or ink from the cut-out areas with the rounded end of a scissor blade. Remove the stencil, trim into a neat oval and your picture will look like multi-coloured stained glass.

Glitter Pictures
These make lovely Christmas or birthday cards, and look very effective against a dark background.

Choose some dark card or thick paper and fold in half to make your card shape. Lay over the stencil and fix it down. Then spread glue all over the cut-out areas - a glue stick is good for this. Take the stencil off the paper and wipe it with a damp cloth to clean off any glue. Then put the card on a larger piece of paper and sprinkle it thickly with glitter.

Tap the card on to the paper to shake off all the spare glitter and leave it to dry for a little while before putting it in an envelope. An adult can help you make the paper into a funnel to pour the extra glitter back in the tube.

Another idea is to draw round the stencils with a glitter or metallic pen. Leave it as a shiny outline or, for an extra sparkly effect, stick on different coloured glitter inside your stencil outline.

Collage
A collage is a picture made out of all sorts of things: pieces of material, magazine pictures, pasta, leaves, feathers and anything interesting you can find around the house! (Ask an adult before you help yourself though.)

Your stencils can be the start of a collage. Paint or crayon a picture you like in the centre of some strong paper or card, leaving a wide border all around it. Then start collecting things to stick on and around the stencil picture. You could surround a picture of Squirrel Nutkin with dried autumn leaves, for example (press them in kitchen paper or blotting paper under some heavy books for couple of days first). Flowers pressed in the same way could be a background for Tom Kitten in the garden, and you could stick on some scraps of material to decorate his clothes. Bark shavings and small seeds would make Mrs. Tittlemouse's store cupboards, and you

could make a pond for Mr. Jeremy Fisher out of some shiny sweet wrappers or kitchen foil.

Stencilling on fabric
A plain T-shirt or handkerchief can be brightened up by a stencilled picture painted with fabric paints or better still, fabric paint "pens" which are easy to use and suit stencilling very well - you can buy Dylon "Color Fun" paints and pens in an art shop or department store.

Wash the piece of clothing first so it is clean and won't shrink or run. Leave it to dry, then lay it out flat on a thick piece of cardboard or pinboard, fixing it down at the corners with drawing pins. (Put a few layers of newspaper inside a T-shirt so that the paints won't run through to the other side.)

Position your stencil and secure it with masking tape. Trace around the inside of your stencil with a soft pencil or tailor's chalk. Remove the stencil and carefully fill in your outlines with fabric paints or colour in with fabric paint pens.

When the paint is dry, ask an adult to iron the fabric from the wrong side with a hot iron.

JOIN THE DOTS

Join the dots to find out who this is.
When you have finished you can paint or colour it in.

FIND THE CLOTHES

Tom Kitten, Mittens and Moppet have been playing in their bedroom. They have made such a mess that they can't find some of their belongings. Unscramble the letters in the words below to find out what they have lost and then find them in the picture. You can paint or colour it in when you have finished.

4 bonribs, 4 tonstub, 1 kocs, 2 soehs

Mrs. Tittlemouse's Tea Party

When she had finished her spring-cleaning, Mrs. Tittlemouse gave a party for her friends. Here are some ideas for food which is fun to make and eat at a party, or any time you feel like something a little bit different! Ask an adult to help you prepare these dishes, especially if you need to use the cooker, and always wash your hands before handling food.

MOUSY BAKED POTATOES

You will need
* 1 potato per person
* butter or margarine
* grated cheese
* tomato ketchup
* slices of raw carrot
* sultanas or golden raisins
* strips of raw carrot

Wash the potatoes, prick with a fork and bake in a medium oven (about 180°C, 350°F, Gas Mark 4) for 40 minutes.

Cut the potatoes in half and scoop the insides into a bowl. The potatoes will be very hot, so hold them in a cloth.

Add a dollop of butter or margarine, some grated cheese and a couple of spoonsful of tomato ketchup. Mash it all together with a fork until the mixture is fairly smooth, then pile it back into the potato halves, making a nice rounded top (the mouse's back).

Ask an adult to grill the filled potatoes until the tops turn golden brown and then arrange them on a plate for you. Turn them into mice by adding carrot slices (cut in half if they are quite big) for ears, and sultanas for the eyes and a nose. Then carefully make a small hole in the bottom of the potato with a knife and stick in a strip of raw carrot for the mouse's tail.

HEDGEHOG ROLLS

You will need:
* white bread mix
* warm water

* a little extra flour
* a little cooking oil
* sultanas
* 1 egg

Use a wooden spoon to stir the bread mix and the water together in a large bowl, following the instructions on the packet to see the right amounts. The water shouldn't be too hot - just nice and warm.

When the mixture is too stiff to stir, use your hands to gather it together into a soft ball. Sprinkle some flour on to a work surface, tip out your dough ball and pummel it for about 5 minutes until it is smooth and stretchy.

Divide the dough into 10 pieces and form them into teardrop shapes with your hands, roughly oval but narrower at one end (the hedgehog's snout). Put them on a greased baking tray, leaving plenty of space

round each one as they will swell up.

Cover the rolls with a damp tea-towel and put them in a warm place for about 20 minutes, until they have risen right up.

Heat oven to 220°C, 425°F, Gas Mark 7.

Snip the dough up into prickles with kitchen scissors along the back of each hedgehog, and press in two sultanas for eyes.

Beat the egg with a fork to mix up the yolk and the white. Brush it over the rolls and bake them in the oven for 12 -15 minutes. Take one out and tap the bottom - if it sounds hollow, the roll is cooked.

BUTTERFLY CAKES

You will need:
* 125 g (4 oz/1 cup) self-raising flour
* 1 tspn (5 ml) baking powder
* 125 g (4 oz) soft tub margarine
* 125 g (4 oz/½ cup) caster sugar
  * 2 eggs
  * a few drops of vanilla essence
    * paper cake cases
    * jam or chocolate spread
    * glacé cherries and
      angelica for
      decoration

Heat oven to 180°C, 350°F, Gas Mark 4.

Sift the flour and the baking powder into a big bowl. Add the margarine, the sugar, the eggs and the vanilla essence, and mix it all together with a wooden spoon or an electric mixer.

Lay out the paper cases on a baking sheet, and fill each one about two-thirds full of cake mixture. Cook for 12-15 minutes, until golden-brown and risen (press the middle of a cake with your finger; if it is ready it will feel springy and your finger won't leave a mark).

Transfer the cakes to a wire rack. When they have cooled, carefully cut a shallow hollow out of the top of each one and fill it with jam or chocolate spread. Cut the circle of cake you have removed in half, and arrange on the jam or spread to look like butterfly wings. Add a slice of glacé cherry for the butterfly body and angelica strips for the antennae.

MARZIPAN FRUIT CAKES

You will need:
* one pack of ready-made marzipan
* red, yellow and green food colouring
* whole cloves or chocolate chips for stalks
* icing (confectioner's) sugar
* lemon juice
* small cakes, made to the recipe above

Divide the marzipan into three and add a few drops of different food colouring to each third. Make the marzipan into tiny bananas, apples, strawberries and oranges (mix red and yellow marzipan together). Press in whole cloves for stalks, or chocolate chips (which don't look as realistic, but which you can eat!).

Mix a medium-sized bowl of icing sugar with a couple of teaspoons of lemon juice until it is as thick as cream.

Spread the icing over the little cakes and, while it is still wet, press in a couple of marzipan fruits.

PARTY DECORATIONS AND GAMES

There are lots of different decorations you can make with your stencils and you can use them for any occasion. Why not hold a Mrs. Tittlemouse party (using the recipes on the previous pages) and coordinate it with a stencil theme. (Refer back to the section on stencilling methods for hints.)

INVITATIONS

Fold some coloured card or thick paper in half to make the card shape.

Tape a stencil over the top and paint or colour a Peter Rabbit picture. Don't forget to write inside when and where your party will be held.

PLACE MATS

Lay a large dinner plate on a sheet of coloured card or thick paper and draw round it with a pencil. Remove the plate and cut round the circle. Then choose a stencil, fix it to the centre of the circle and paint or colour it in. With a thick pen or paints, write the name of your guest around

the top edge - colour and decorate as you wish. Do the same for all your friends and when you lay the table for your party everyone will know where they will be sitting.

TABLE DECORATIONS

Continue the stencil theme with these table decorations. You'll need card, scissors, paints or pens.

Stencil a character on to the centre of a sheet of card with paints or coloured pens. Cut around the edges of the shape, leaving a rectangle roughly 4 cm deep and several centimetres wider than your stencil character at the bottom for a base. Then make a 2 cm cut at the centre bottom of this base.

Cut a matching base from another piece of card the same length and width as the base of your decoration, and make another cut, as before, about 2 cm deep.

Now slot this rectangle at right angles to the base of your decoration at the cuts, making a cross shape of the two bases. Your table decoration should now stand firmly.

STENCIL HATS AND CROWNS

You can also make each of your friends a stencilled hat or crown to wear at your party. You'll need thin card or paper, scissors, tape, coloured pens or paints and a tape measure or piece of string for measuring your head.

Ask an adult to help you measure around your head with a tape measure or length of string. Now cut a strip of thin card or paper about 6 cm deep and several centimetres longer than the size or your head.

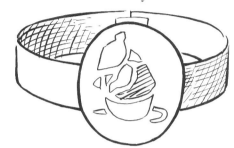

Hats

Now stencil a character on to a separate piece of card and cut neatly around the outline of the shape. Stick this shape on to the centre of your paper strip with glue.

Tape the ends of the strip together (with a little overlap) to make a ring large enough to fit your head.

Crowns

Follow the instructions for the hat, but instead of a plain strip of card, cut neat triangles along the length of one edge to look like a crown.

Using your small stencils, colour little characters along this strip and again fasten the two ends with tape.

Because you have used tape to stick the ends together, if the hat is a little too big or small for some of your friends you can easily readjust the size.

PARTY FRIEZE

Stencil lots of different characters on to paper. Trim around the outlines and using a hole-punch, make a hole at the top centre of each. String them on to a length of cord or string and between each tie ribbons, streamers or tinsel.

You can pin your frieze around the edges of a table, or hang it from a wall.

GAMES

Pin the Tail on Peter Rabbit

Draw a rabbit on to a large sheet of card or paper, but don't give him a tail. (You might prefer to ask an adult to do the drawing for you.) Stick a piece of double-sided sticky tape to a cotton-wool ball to make a tail (make enough tails for every player). Each player is blindfolded in turn and has to stick their tail as near as they can to the right place on the rabbit. The person closest wins.

Mr. Jeremy's Racing Fish

Cut fish shapes out of thin paper or newspaper. Give all the players a magazine and you are now ready to start a fishy race.

Everyone lines up at the end of the room and on the word "go", each player wafts their fish along with a magazine. The first fish over the finishing line is the winner.

Sleeping Bunnies

Ask an adult to be the referee. All the players must lie on the floor and pretend to be sleeping. Anyone who moves, twitches or shuffles is out, and the last player in is the winning sleeping bunny.

WORD SQUARE

Hidden in this word square are 24 things to be found in and around Mr. Jeremy Fisher's pond. They can be read across, backwards and diagonally - see if you can find them all. One word has been found already and to help you all the words are listed below.

water	trout	rat	rain	worm	snail
stickleback	dragonfly	lily	minnow	fish	tree
duck	grass	buttercup	rushes	leaves	beetle
stones	mud	frog	ripple	reeds	pondweed

W	A	T	E	R	K	W	R	X	F	M	R	O	W	K
H	B	U	C	A	B	S	N	A	I	L	I	D	E	C
D	F	O	E	T	I	T	I	J	I	I	E	C	G	H
R	S	R	U	V	L	I	L	Y	C	N	M	M	S	W
A	C	T	B	Y	R	C	A	S	E	U	J	I	X	B
G	F	H	D	U	C	K	E	D	E	F	F	N	Z	U
O	S	S	A	R	G	L	E	A	R	N	V	N	K	T
N	P	H	R	T	R	E	M	D	T	W	R	O	M	T
F	K	L	M	S	W	B	W	C	H	U	G	W	T	E
L	R	E	E	D	S	A	D	P	S	N	O	R	S	R
Y	I	B	N	Z	C	C	F	H	Q	E	B	Y	H	C
T	P	O	R	K	M	K	E	G	J	Y	V	V	K	U
P	P	F	R	O	G	S	Q	Z	X	O	W	A	R	P
X	L	W	H	J	B	F	R	B	E	E	T	L	E	X
S	E	F	D	U	M	S	W	S	E	N	O	T	S	L

18

MRS. TITTLEMOUSE MAZE

Mother Ladybird, the big fat spider, Babbitty Bumble and Mr. Jackson are all lost in Mrs. Tittlemouse's home with its yards of sandy passages. Can you find out which character has chosen the one clear path to the bank outside?

PETER RABBIT PUPPETS AND THEATRE

Puppets are lots of fun to make and play with; you can act out the stories of Peter Rabbit and his friends, or make up new ones. Here are some easy ways to make puppets and also a theatre to go with the push-on figures described below.
(Refer to the stencilling methods section to help you out.)

FINGER PUPPETS

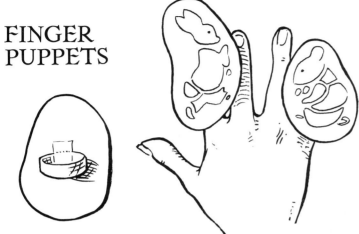

Stencil some Peter Rabbit characters on to white card. Then ask an adult to help you cut round each figure. Cut a thin strip of cardboard and then tape the ends together to make a ring, large enough to fit your finger through. Tape the ring to the back of the characters you have stencilled and use your finger to make him or her move. These finger puppets are ideal to play with on a table or the floor.

PUSH-ON PUPPETS

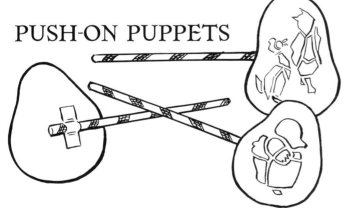

Stencil some Peter Rabbit characters on to white card. Then ask an adult to help you cut round each figure and tape a plastic drinking straw or a plant support stick to the back (this is the handle which you'll use to make your puppet move). Make sure some straws go to the left and some to the

right because these puppets can be used in your theatre and they will need to come on to the stage from each side.

PUPPET THEATRE

You will need:
* a medium-sized strong cardboard box - a large cereal or washing powder box is ideal
* some white paper and card
* craft knife
* ruler
* scissors
* glue
* sticky tape
* a pencil and paints or felt tip pens

Reseal any open flaps of the box with tape. Ask an adult to help you cut out three sides of the box with a craft knife following the diagram below. Leave plenty of margin around the top and sides of the theatre front so you'll have lots of space for decoration.

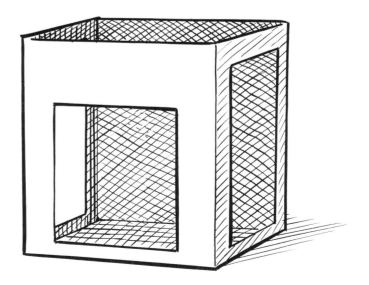

Cut out the top of the box completely, but leave about a 2 cm margin around each edge of the sides - this will help to keep the box strong and in shape. (The two sides you haven't cut will be the floor and back of your theatre).

Now you are ready to decorate the front of your theatre.

Cut a large semi-circle out of card the same width as the top of your theatre. Use your small stencils to decorate and use pens or paints to write the name of your theatre around the top edge. Finish off with dramatic swirls and flourishes.

Stick this semi-circle with glue to the top of your theatre front and decorate the outside of your theatre as you wish. You can use some of the ideas from the diagram using collage, pens and paints or use your imagination and your stencils.

Scenery

Now you can think about what scenery you want to use - you can paint or colour a scene straight on to the back of the theatre or you can make a variety of backgrounds. Draw different scenes on further sheets of white cardboard slightly smaller than the back of your theatre. Tape drinking straws to the top of each backdrop at the right and left hand edges, so that they rest on the top of the box frame.

Curtain

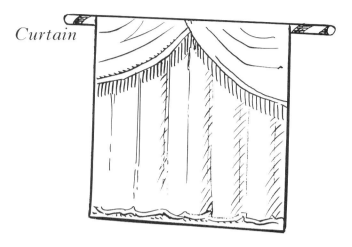

Use this same principle to make a curtain. Again, take a sheet of card slightly smaller than the back of your theatre and draw on bright red curtains with pens or paints. Tape drinking straws to the top at the right and left hand edges so it rests on the top of the box frame. You can then raise and lower your curtain at the beginning and end of your performance and between scene changes.

Now you are ready to put on your own Peter Rabbit play. Look at Beatrix Potter's little books to give you ideas for storylines, or make up your own. Let the play begin!

STENCIL MOBILE

You will need:
* card
* scissors
* pens or paints
* a wooden embroidery hoop 15 cm
 (6 in) in diameter
* some white cord or ribbon

Stencil four different characters on to pieces of card with pens or paints (see the stencilling methods section). Cut around the outlines of your stencils.

Cut four pieces of cord, each ½ m (½ yd) long. Fold a length of cord in half to find the middle, tie round the hoop and knot so that you have two equal lengths of cord hanging from the hoop. Do this with the other three lengths of cord, equal distances apart. Attach the stencils to four of the hanging cords with sticky tape at the back and tie the four remaining loose cords together with a knot at the top.

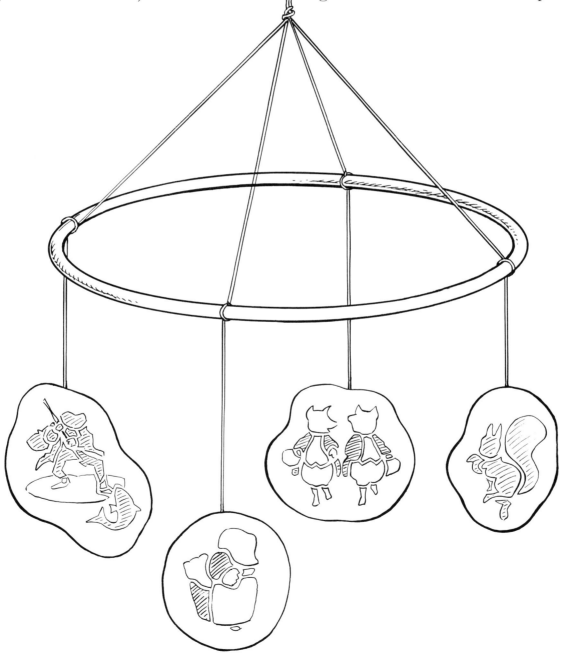

LOVE FROM BENJAMIN

Benjamin Bunny has a plan for himself and his cousin Peter Rabbit which he doesn't want anyone else to know about. Can you work out this picture note which Benjamin has slipped into Peter's burrow?

Dear Peter,

Love from

ANSWERS TO PUZZLES

GINGER AND PICKLES CROSSWORD

Down
1. wall
2. soap
3. hungry
4. purse
5. tom
6. rat
7. office
8. half
9. bed
10. candles
11. Pickles

Across
1. wag
2. sugar
3. bill
4. and 12. on, counter
5. apron
6. toffee
7. mice
8. hen
9. bark
10. add
11. cash
12. see 4. above

MR. JEREMY WORD SQUARE

W	A	T	E	R	K	W	R	X	F	M	R	O	W	K
H	B	U	C	A	B	S	N	A	I	L	I	D	E	C
D	F	O	E	T	I	P	I	J	I	E	C	G	H	
R	S	R	U	V	L	I	L	Y	C	N	M	M	S	W
A	C	T	B	Y	R	C	A	S	E	U	J	I	X	B
G	F	H	D	U	C	K	E	D	E	F	F	N	Z	U
O	S	S	A	R	G	I	E	A	R	N	V	N	K	T
N	P	H	R	T	R	E	M	D	T	W	R	O	M	T
F	K	L	M	S	W	B	W	C	H	U	G	W	T	E
L	R	E	E	D	S	A	D	P	S	N	O	R	S	R
Y	I	B	N	Z	C	C	F	H	Q	E	B	Y	H	C
T	P	O	R	K	M	K	E	G	J	Y	V	V	K	U
P	P	F	R	O	G	S	Q	Z	X	O	W	A	R	P
X	L	W	H	J	B	F	R	B	E	E	T	L	E	X
S	E	F	D	U	M	S	W	S	E	N	O	T	S	L

FIND THE CLOTHES

The missing things are:
4 ribbons, 4 buttons, 1 sock, 2 shoes

MRS. TITTLEMOUSE MAZE

Babbitty Bumble has the clear path

LOVE FROM BENJAMIN

Dear Peter,

How would you like to go to Mr. McGregor's garden again? I saw Mr. McGregor go off to town this morning in the pony-cart, so we can climb down the pear tree again, to look for some onions. Don't let your mother know what we're up to, or she will be cross. Meet me at the wall in half an hour.

Love from Benjamin.